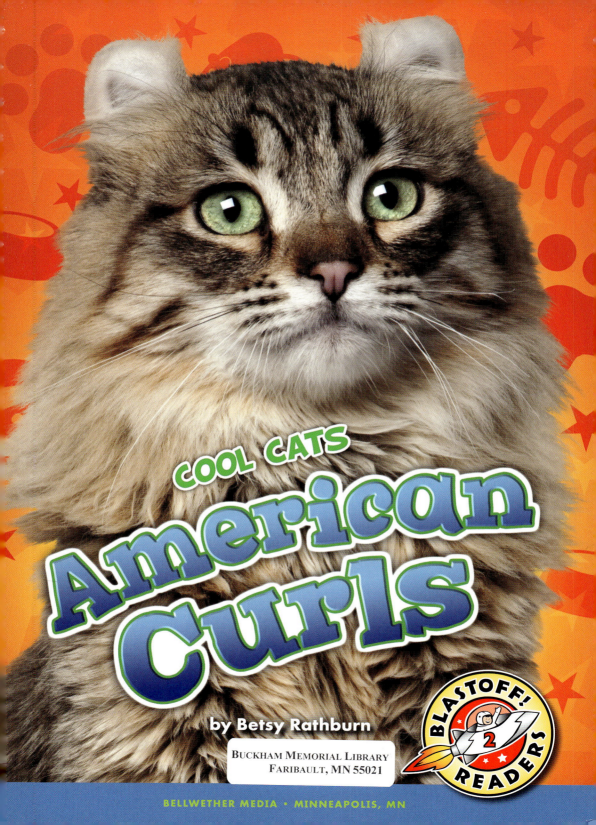

Note to Librarians, Teachers, and Parents:

Blastoff! Readers are carefully developed by literacy experts and combine standards-based content with developmentally appropriate text.

Level 1 provides the most support through repetition of high-frequency words, light text, predictable sentence patterns, and strong visual support.

Level 2 offers early readers a bit more challenge through varied simple sentences, increased text load, and less repetition of high-frequency words.

Level 3 advances early-fluent readers toward fluency through increased text and concept load, less reliance on visuals, longer sentences, and more literary language.

Level 4 builds reading stamina by providing more text per page, increased use of punctuation, greater variation in sentence patterns, and increasingly challenging vocabulary.

Level 5 encourages children to move from "learning to read" to "reading to learn" by providing even more text, varied writing styles, and less familiar topics.

Whichever book is right for your reader, Blastoff! Readers are the perfect books to build confidence and encourage a love of reading that will last a lifetime!

This edition first published in 2018 by Bellwether Media, Inc.

No part of this publication may be reproduced in whole or in part without written permission of the publisher. For information regarding permission, write to Bellwether Media, Inc., Attention: Permissions Department, 5357 Penn Avenue South, Minneapolis, MN 55419.

Library of Congress Cataloging-in-Publication Data

Names: Rathburn, Betsy, author.
Title: American Curls / by Betsy Rathburn.
Description: Minneapolis, MN : Bellwether Media, Inc., 2018. | Series: Blastoff! Readers. Cool Cats | Includes bibliographical references and index. | Audience: Ages 5 to 8. | Audience: Grades K to 3.
Identifiers: LCCN 2016052712 (print) | LCCN 2017002210 (ebook) | ISBN 9781626176256 (hardcover : alk. paper) | ISBN 9781681033556 (ebook)
Subjects: LCSH: American curl cat–Juvenile literature.
Classification: LCC SF449.A44 R38 2018 (print) | LCC SF449.A44 (ebook) | DDC 636.8/3–dc23
LC record available at https://lccn.loc.gov/2016052712

Text copyright © 2018 by Bellwether Media, Inc. BLASTOFF! READERS and associated logos are trademarks and/or registered trademarks of Bellwether Media, Inc. SCHOLASTIC, CHILDREN'S PRESS, and associated logos are trademarks and/or registered trademarks of Scholastic Inc.

Editor: Nathan Sommer   Designer: Lois Stanfield

Printed in the United States of America, North Mankato, MN.

Table of Contents

What Are American Curls?	4
History of American Curls	8
Curled and Colorful	12
Friendly and Frisky	18
Glossary	22
To Learn More	23
Index	24

What Are American Curls?

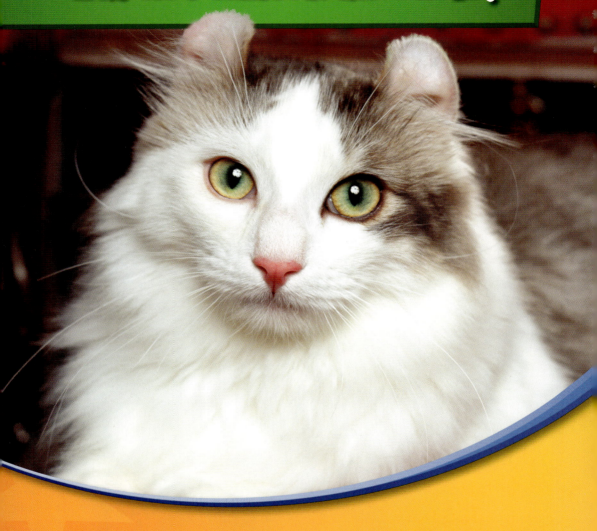

American curls are lovable cats with **distinct** looks.

They are named for their unusual ears. These curl backward toward their heads.

American curls are fun to be around. Many greet visitors at the door.

These cats love when people pet their **silky** fur!

History of American Curls

In 1981, Californians Joe and Grace Ruga found a cat with curled ears. They named her Shulamith.

Shulamith had two curly-eared kittens. This started the new **breed**!

Soon, more curly-eared cats were **bred** to have the same look.

Today, American curls are loved pets.

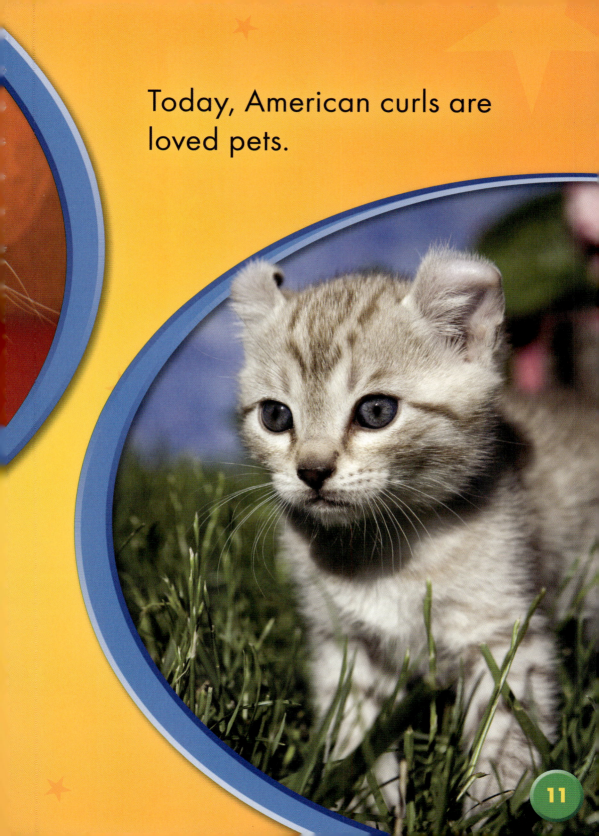

Curled and Colorful

American curl kittens are born with straight ears. These begin to curl soon after birth.

The ears stop curling when the kittens are about four months old.

American curls have large, walnut-shaped eyes. These can be any color. The cats have medium-sized bodies with soft, shiny fur.

American Curl Profile

curled ears ——

walnut-shaped eyes ——

silky fur ———

Weight: 5 to 10 pounds (2 to 5 kilograms)

Life Span: 12 to 16 years

American curls can have short or long **coats**. The coats come in many colors and patterns.

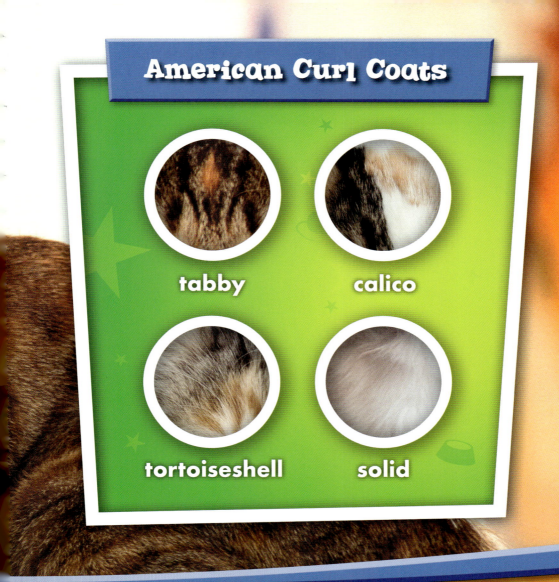

Tabby and **calico** are popular patterns. **Tortoiseshell** is also common.

Friendly and Frisky

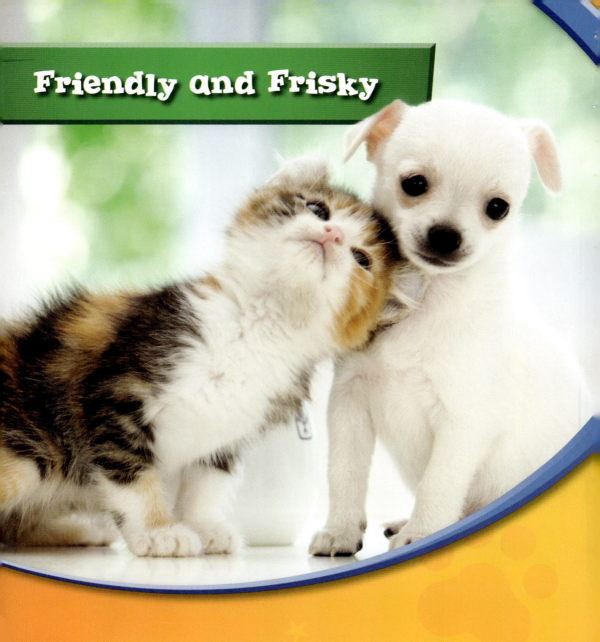

American curls are social cats. They get along well with other pets and children.

They love to climb onto laps to nap and purr.

When they feel **frisky**, American curls chase after toys.

They are sometimes called Peter Pan cats. Many play like kittens for their entire lives!

Glossary

bred—purposely mated two cats to make kittens with certain qualities

breed—a type of cat

calico—a pattern that has patches of white, black, and reddish brown fur

coats—the hair or fur covering some animals

distinct—clearly recognizable

frisky—playful and lively

silky—soft, smooth, and shiny

tabby—a pattern that has stripes, patches, or swirls of colors

tortoiseshell—a pattern of yellow, orange, and black with few or no patches of white

To Learn More

AT THE LIBRARY
Finne, Stephanie. *American Curl Cats*. Minneapolis, Minn.: Checkerboard Library, 2015.

Hengel, Katherine. *Amazing American Curls*. Edina, Minn.: ABDO, 2012.

Leaf, Christina. *Scottish Folds*. Minneapolis, Minn.: Bellwether Media, 2016.

ON THE WEB
Learning more about American curls is as easy as 1, 2, 3.

1. Go to www.factsurfer.com.

2. Enter "American curls" into the search box.

3. Click the "Surf" button and you will see a list of related web sites.

With factsurfer.com, finding more information is just a click away.

Index

bodies, 14
bred, 10
breed, 9
California, 8
chase, 20
children, 18
climb, 19
coats, 16, 17
colors, 16
ears, 5, 8, 9, 10, 12, 13, 15
eyes, 14, 15
fur, 7, 14, 15
greet, 6
kittens, 9, 12, 13, 21
life span, 15
name, 5

nap, 19
nickname, 21
patterns, 16, 17
pets, 11, 18
purr, 19
Ruga, Grace, 8
Ruga, Joe, 8
Shulamith, 8, 9
size, 14, 15
toys, 20
visitors, 6

The images in this book are reproduced through the courtesy of: Eric Isselee, front cover, pp. 9 (subjects), 15, 17 (lower left), 20; Ron Kimball/ KimballStock, pp. 4-5; Helmi Flick/ Helmi Flick Cat Photography, pp. 5, 8; Astrid Harrisson/ Alamy, pp. 6, 14-15, 17 (upper right, lower right); Evannovostro, p. 7 (subjects); Room27, p. 7 (background); Everything, p. 9 (background); Tierfotoagentur/ R. Richter/ Age Fotostock, pp. 10-11, 20-21; Robynrg, p. 11; Linn Currie, p. 12; Zanna Holstova, pp. 12-13; Juniors Bildarchiv GmbH/ Alamy, pp. 16-17, 17 (upper left); Yoshio Tomii/ KimballStock, pp. 18-19; Alex Milan Tracy/ Sipa USA/ Newscom, p. 19.

24